YOUR KNOWLEDGE H

- We will publish your bachelor's and master's thesis, essays and papers

- Your own eBook and book - sold worldwide in all relevant shops

- Earn money with each sale

Upload your text at www.GRIN.com and publish for free

Alexandra Koch

Edmund Burke's Theory of the Sublime and It's Reflection in Gothic Fiction: Mary Shelley's "Frankenstein"

GRIN Verlag

Bibliografische Information der Deutschen Nationalbibliothek:

Die Deutsche Bibliothek verzeichnet diese Publikation in der Deutschen National-
bibliografie; detaillierte bibliografische Daten sind im Internet über http://dnb.d-
nb.de/ abrufbar.

Imprint:

Copyright © 2011 GRIN Verlag GmbH
Druck und Bindung: Books on Demand GmbH, Norderstedt Germany
ISBN: 978-3-656-25289-4

This book at GRIN:

http://www.grin.com/en/e-book/198423/edmund-burke-s-theory-of-the-sublime-
and-it-s-reflection-in-gothic-fiction

GRIN - Your knowledge has value

Der GRIN Verlag publiziert seit 1998 wissenschaftliche Arbeiten von Studenten, Hochschullehrern und anderen Akademikern als eBook und gedrucktes Buch. Die Verlagswebsite www.grin.com ist die ideale Plattform zur Veröffentlichung von Hausarbeiten, Abschlussarbeiten, wissenschaftlichen Aufsätzen, Dissertationen und Fachbüchern.

Visit us on the internet:

http://www.grin.com/

http://www.facebook.com/grincom

http://www.twitter.com/grin_com

<u>Proseminar term paper</u>

RWTH Aachen

Department of English, American and Romance Intercultural Studies

Chair of English Literary Studies

Topic:

EDMUND BURKE'S THEORY OF THE SUBLIME

AND ITS REFLECTION IN GOTHIC FICTION:

MARY SHELLEY'S *FRANKENSTEIN*

Seminar instructor:

...

Proseminar: Gothic Literature

SS 2011

By:

...

Englisch (Gym./Ges.)

05 August 2011, Aachen

TABLE OF CONTENTS

1. INTRODUCTION

Many authors would agree that *Frankenstein* is one of the most famous Gothic tales of all time. It was first published in 1818 and is famous for its descriptions of landscape and nature, as well as its prophetic dimension. More than 60 years before the novel was published, Edmund Burke set out to analyze the sublime. By doing so, he actually took an important step towards founding the genre Shelley engaged in, in writing *Frankenstein*. His *A Philosophical Inquiry into the Origins of our Ideas of the Beautiful and the Sublime* published in 1757 became a great success.

This term paper sets out to shed light on a number of problem areas concerning the connection between Shelley's novel and Burke's theory of the sublime. The paper arose out of the Proseminar 'Gothic Literatur' by XY, M.A. in the Summer Semester 2011 at RWTH University Aachen. During the course, different topics concerning the Gothic novel were discussed in combination with four of the most famous novels belonging to the genre. Among them was *Frankenstein* as a novel and 'Burke's Theory of the Sublime and Its Reflection in the Gothic Fiction' as a topic.

The central question to be examined in this paper is how Burke's theory of the sublime is reflected in Shelley's Gothic novel. Further questions to be dealt with in this term paper are: what is the Burkean sublime? What was new and different about Burke's concept of the Sublime – as the Sublime itself is by no means a groundbreaking, new concept. Does Shelley intentionally incorporate sublime features in her novel or comment on the use of Burke's theory? Is there a social dimension to Burke's theory? In what way does the novel reflect the sublime? Is a sense of the sublime only conveyed through descriptions of nature? Or, are there studies that suggest a sublime that goes beyond this surface? Finally, to what way is the monster important with regard to Burke's theory?

The paper presented here is based on Edmund Burke's 1757 published *A Philosophical Inquiry into the Origins of our Ideas of the Beautiful and the Sublime* and, of course, on Mary Shelly's *Frankenstein. Or, The Modern Prometheus*. In addition, it takes into account James Sambrooks chapter "Aesthetics" published in Sambrook's *The Eighteenth Century. The Intellectual and Cultural Context of English Literature, 1700 – 1789*, which, in general, draws together Burke's main ideas on the sublime. The same does Alison Milbank's article "The Sublime", Sage's article on the "Gothic Novel" and Ingeborg Weber's *Edmund Burkes Ästhetik des Erhabenen als Gattungspoetik des englischen Schauerromans*. Also, Paola Giacomoni's argumentation in "Mountain landscape and the aesthetics of the sublime in Roman-

1

tic narration", published in *Romantic prose fiction* and Frederick's in *On the Sublime and Beautiful in Shelley's Frankenstein* are part of the paper presented here.

The first part of the term paper presents Burke's theory of the sublime, an analysis of the connection between Shelley and the sublime and an analysis of the social dimension of the sublime. The next part is going to shed light on how Frankenstein as a Gothic novel reflects elements of Burke's theory of the sublime. A fuller discussion including an analysis of all scenes displaying sublime elements would go beyond the range of the paper. In this matter only five scenes were chosen. Those scenes are significant for the plot development, as well as they help to support the line of argumentation. Eventually, a conclusion will be drawn.

The analysis of the text abstracts will, hopefully, help to exemplify how a sense of the sublime, as described in Burke's *Inquiry*, is conveyed in Shelley's Gothic novel.

2. THE SUBLIME

2.1 BURKE'S THEORY OF THE SUBLIME

The concept of the Sublime dates back to ancient Greek, to be more specific to Longinus's[1] *Peri Hypsous*. But did – despite several translations and reprints from the 16th century on – not in particular gain interest until Boileau's translation into French in 1674. (cf. Lamb 1997: 394) In Britain the concept finally established after Welsted's translation in 1712 and Smith's *Dionysius Longinus on the Sublime* in 1739. The theory widened and diversified over time and especially in the lively aesthetic debate in Europe in the 18th century. And when Burke in 1757 published his twist on the Sublime – *A Philosophical Inquiry into the origins of the Beautiful and Sublime* – he was one among many to deal with the theory of the Sublime. (cf. ibid., 394)

Burke, as literature widely agrees, may well be seen as the father of Gothic Sublimity or as Ingeborg Weber puts it, he was a "Gattungspoetiker[s]"[2] (Weber 1983: 23). (cf. ibid., 23) Alison Milbank agrees in her article on the sublime and states that "Burke provides a psychological justification for the Gothic tale of terror" (Milbank 1998: 227) by basing it on Locke's psychology and by provoking man's natural instinct to preserve his own existence. (cf. Weber 1983: 23; cf. Milbank 1998: 227) As shown, it can be indubitably stated that Burke's work has had a profound influence on the conception of Gothic Fiction. As Ingeborg Weber declare's, Burke's sublime is "eine Manifestation des ästhetischen Paradigmenwechsels vom Klassizismus zur Romantik, in dessen Konsequenz der englische Schauerroman entstand [.]" (Weber 1983: 20) Burke's theory builds a jumping-off point for the development of the 18th century Gothic fiction.

As the title *A Philosophical Inquiry into the origins of the Beautiful and Sublime* suggests, Burke obviously differentiates between "two classes of agreeable sensations" (Sambrook 1986: 121): the beautiful and the sublime. In this section the content of the term paper will be the sublime. The beautiful will be dealt with among other things in the section on the social dimension of the sublime.

When looking at Burke's *A Philosophical Inquiry into the origins of the Beautiful and Sublime*, one can see that Burke defines the sublime in general as "productive of strongest emotion, which the mind is capable of feeling" (Burke 1757). He furthermore states, "[w]hatever is fitted in any sort to excite the ideas of pain, and danger, that is to say, whatever

---

[1] There is some evidence to suggest that *Peri Huospus* is falsely accredited to Longinus. In literature it is even referred to the author as Pseudo-Longinus. (cf. Weber 1983: 20; cf. Milbank 1998: 226) But for a lack of alternatives, this paper refers to the author as Longinus.
[2] For lack of a corresponding English literary term, the German term is used here.

3

is in any sort terrible, or is conversant about terrible objects, or operates in a manner analogous to terror, is a source of the sublime [.]" (Burke 1757) Burke also says that "[n]o so effectually robs the mind of all its powers of acting and reasoning as *fear.* [...] Whatever therefore is terrible, with regard to sight, is sublime too [.]" (ibid.). Especially important with regard to fear, Burke states, is obscurity and uncertainty because "[t]o make anything very terrible, obscurity seems in general to be necessary." (ibid.) Sambrook specifies Burke's idea of terror by saying that it is a "distanced or modified terror" (Sambrook 1986: 121).

Burke takes special interest in the affects pain and pleasure. They build the basis for his theory. Burke argues that there are two independent types of pain and two independent types of pleasure: 'positive pain' and 'positive pleasure', and 'pain as removal of pleasure', also described as 'grief', and 'pleasure as removal of pain', also called 'delight'. (cf. Weber 1983: 25 – 26) 'Positive pain' and 'positive pleasure' differ from 'grief' and 'delight'. 'Grief' and 'delight' are mixed emotions. For example, 'delight' "is that pleasure which arises from the ideas of pain and danger when we are not in actual pain and danger" (ibid., 121), as Sambrook expresses. Burke justifies that 'delight' is the source of the sublime as it is essential for the human psyche as it can trigger powerful feelings of both pain and pleasure. (cf. Weber 1983: 26) As Weber states, this phenomenon according to Burke, is called '*delightful horror*'. (cf. ibid., 22)

In the *Philosophical Inquiry*, Burke basically presents an analysis of various characteristics of things that the Sublime can be associated with; these are called stimuli. (cf. Weber 1983: 37; cf. Milbank 1998: 228) Stimuli are triggering 'delight'. They can be: 'god', 'death', 'loneliness', 'pain', 'strength', 'violence', 'grandeur', 'vastness', 'infinity', 'terror', 'obscurity/uncertainty', 'difficulty, disorder', 'magnificence', 'silence', 'vanity' and 'succession'. Opposite extremes such as 'vastness' and 'littleness', 'excessive loudness' and 'utter silence' and 'darkness' and 'extreme light' can function as stimuli as well. (cf. ibid. 37; cf. ibid. 228)

Concluding this section, we can say that Burke's analysis of the sublime is

"founded on an aesthetics of process, foregrounding the affective relationship between reader and text. Burke's treatise is a blueprint for an aesthetics of terror and horror, laying down a set of conditions for the excitement of the reader's passions. The writer's task was to evoke fear, grandeur and awe in the soul of the reader." (Sage 1998: 82)

2.2 SHELLEY AND THE SUBLIME

Mary Shelley followed these principles in writing *Frankenstein*. As Mary Shelley puts it in her Introduction to *Frankenstein* from 1831:

I busied myself to *think of a story* [...][,][o]ne which would speak to the mysterious fears of our nature and awaken thrilling horror – one to make the reader dread to look round, to curdle the blood, and quicken the beatings of the heart. (Shelley 1994: 7 – 8)

Mary Shelly is widely considered a Romantic writer. But as many Romantic writers in this time, Mary Shelley engaged in writing Gothic fiction. (cf. Martin 1998: 197) By writing the Gothic novel *Frankenstein*, she actually followed the tradition of her parents, who both wrote amongst other things novels influenced by Gothicism. (cf. ibid., 199) In general, it can be added that "Romanticism and Gothicism are inter-related in many ways" (ibid.,196). Therefore it is no coincidence that Romantic writers chose the Gothic Genre to engage writing in.

Shelley's novel *Frankenstein* is generally considered "unequivocally Gothic in Style" (Martin 1998: 197). The novel, according to Martin, "shows a strong dependence on Gothic conventions" (ibid. 199). This is especially true with regard to narrative technique and the themes used in the novel, and, of course, by incorporating the sublime and beautiful, Martin argues. (cf. ibid. 199)

Especially interesting is Nancy Fredericks argumentation in her article *On the sublime and beautiful in Shelley's Frankenstein*. She argues that in Shelley's Introduction to *Frankenstein* from 1831 Shelley links "the discourse of the sublime [...] to scenes of empowerment [...] and emerge[s] of her literary voice" (Fredericks 1996) She summarizes Shelley's Introduction and then concludes that "[t]he sublime provides the setting for her imaginative release from the enslavement of mimesis and the world of the senses." (ibid.) And furthermore, she argues that in the introduction, Shelley "presents [...] [a] sublime setting, the stormy Swiss Alps where Shelley conceives of the story of *Frankenstein*." (ibid.) Fredericks argues that the inspiration for *Frankenstein* is the real sublime Shelley experienced in the Swiss Alps. Although this is an interesting assumption, it sadly lacks evidence and can be seen critical.

Finally, it can be stated that the Gothic novel, in general, was a phenomenon that rose against the background of 18th century Enlightenment; an era known for Protestantism, rationalism and scientific progress. All the more interesting is the flourishing of the catholic influenced Gothic Novel, dealing with supernatural occurrences, usually set in a medieval setting, and, of course, influenced by Edmund Burke's 1757 published theory of the Sublime. (cf. Sage 1998: 81 – 82)

Concluding this section, it can be stated that Mary Shelley, although a Romantic writer, challenged herself to write the Gothic novel *Frankenstein*. She was one among many Romantic writers that published also Gothic fiction Especially in her introduction to the novel from 1831, features that lead to the conclusion that she was aware of Burke's concept and intentionally engage in writing a novel that had an according affect on the reader can be found.

2.3 THE SOCIAL DIMENSION OF THE SUBLIME

When looking at Sambrook's article "Aesthetics", it becomes clear that Burke's *Philosophical Inquiry* also has a political dimension to it. Sambrook contrasts the sublime from the beautiful by saying that it "suggests a distinction of social categories." (Sambrook 1986: 121) The sublime, in contrast to the beautiful, is derived from 'delight' which "is a selfish passion [...] and is our response to the sublime" (ibid., 121). The beautiful, on the other hand, arises from 'positive pleasure' and is therefore "a social passion and is our emotional response to the beautiful" (ibid., 121). Thereby the category of the beautiful is "including all the regular and soft qualities that Burke considers feminine." (Milbank 1998: 227)

Burke distinguishes the beautiful from the sublime as followed,

"They are indeed ideas of a very different nature, one being founded on pain, the other on pleasure; and however they may vary afterwards from the direct nature of their causes, yet these causes keep up an eternal distinction between them, a distinction never to be forgotten by any whose business it is to affect the passions." (Burke 1757)

and also:

"I call beauty a social quality; for where women and men, and not only they, but when other animals give us a sense of joy and pleasure in beholding them (and there are many that do so), they inspire us with sentiments of tenderness and affection towards their persons; we like to have them near us, and we enter willingly into a kind of relation with them, unless we should have strong reasons to the contrary." (Burke 1757)

Beauty in contrast to the sublime is consequently an essential part of the human relationships and constitution of society. (cf. Weber 1983: 27 – 28) The sublime, on the other hand, is merely "arising from our instincts for self-preservation" (Sambrook 1986: 121). It might even be argued that to some degree the beautiful and the sublime can be seen as representatives of the society and the individual, as Weber states. She subsequently dismisses the thought due to Burke's definition of the concept of 'sympathy'. (cf. Weber 1983: 28)

To summarize, it can be said that the sublime and the beautiful differ profoundly. The beautiful is generally considered as a social category and necessary for the co-existence of individuals in societies.

6

3. THE REFLECTION OF THE SUBLIME IN FRANKENSTEIN

The following section sets out to examine the reflection of the sublime in Mary Shelley's novel *Frankenstein*. In the first part, it is explored in length how the Alps are often seen as a large part of how Burke's sublime is conveyed in the novel. Also, Victor's perception of the sublime will be discussed. And, in addition, further sublime settings such as the glacier and the arctic realm, are taken into account as well. Finally, the connection between Burke's conception of the beautiful with its social dimension and *Frankenstein*'s reflection of the beautiful and the outcasts are compared briefly and exemplarily.

Martin states in his article on Romanticism that the alpine environment represents a large part of how a sense of the sublime is conveyed in *Frankenstein*. (cf. Martin 1998: 199) Similarly, Giacomoni argues in her article "Mountain landscape and the aesthetics of the sublime in Romantic narration", that the recurrent appearance of mountains which at first seem to be "a place of recognition and of peacefulness" (Giacomoni 2008: 120) repeatedly turn to the opposite very quickly. They then appear dark and dangerous. (cf. ibid., 120) The scene with the encounter between the monster and Frankenstein on Victor's return to Geneva after his brother William was found dead, murdered by the monster, is an good example for this. (cf. appendix 1. Encounter of Victor and the monster on his return to Geneva after his brother William was found murdered) Text abstract (1) indicates the sudden change from Victor's familiar and beloved countryside to a "scene of evil" (Shelley 1994: 72), dark and vast, essentially a reflection of Burke's conception of the sublime. As the scene moves on (text abstract (2)), the play of the lightning in the dark on the top of Mont Blanc, shows another reflection of the sublime conveyed through darkness and extreme light in combination with the vastness and magnificence of the Mont Blanc. As the scene enhances, Victor describes the storm as "so beautiful, yet terrific" (ibid., 73), thereby actually capturing the essence of Burke's sublime, 'delight'.

As a result of this shift, occurring also in the scene at the lake after Victor and Elizabeth got married, Giacomoni argues that nature appears to be conflicted because it is "both calming and at the same time disturbing" (Giacomoni 2008: 120) Giacomoni furthermore argues that this confliction is also reflected in Frankenstein himself. (cf. ibid., 120) She states that "[t]he landscape clearly symbolizes Frankenstein's ambivalence, his thirst for knowledge and his hubis, which diffuses the impetus in the deformed and the monstrous" (ibid,. 120).

Giacomoni also approaches the sublime landscape of the Alps from Victor's point of view, for he is the narrator for large parts of the novel (alongside Walton and the monster).

She argues that the mountain landscape "neither depresses nor rejects him" (ibid., 119). "Nature appears to be 'maternal' and consequently makes him feel 'waited on' and tranquillised." (Giacomoni 2008, 119) She advances by saying that "[a]ccording to [Victor], the awful element itself and the sublime do not connect to an idea of destruction and decline, but to one of duration as well as eternity." (ibid., 119) The text abstracts of scene "2. Travel to the glacier" of the appendix, convey the here-described effect on Victor Frankenstein. The landscape is described in length and necessarily through Victor's eyes. The implied vastness in comparison to Victor seize as a sole individual is ubiquitously. The vastness and magnificence of the scene, as described by Victor, conveys a sense of a sublime originating in natural phenomenon, as described by Burke. Victor is clearly moved and affected by this sight as he refers to both, the Alps (text abstract (6)) and the valley (text abstract (7)), as sublime. (cf. appendix 2. Travel to the glacier) In scene "3. Face-to-face encounter with the monster on the top of the glacier", text abstract (8), Victor's disposition triggered by the sight is articulated as followed,

> "[t]hese sublime and magnificence scenes afforded me the greatest consolation that I was capable of receiving. They elevated me from all littleness of feeling, and although they did not remove my grief, they subdued and tranquillized it. In some degree, also, they diverted my mind from the thoughts over which it had brooded for the last month. (Shelley 1994: 92; emphasis mine, A.K.)

Burke's sublime, defined as "productive of the strongest feelings the mind is capable of feeling" (Burke 1757), is clearly visible. Up until this moment Victor was not able to distract his mind from the past events. Only in the presence of the sublime of the Alps and the valley, he is able to forget. (cf. Shelley 1994: 92)

Giacomoni and Fredericks (in her article *On the sublime and beautiful in Shelley's Frankenstein*) additionally step beyond the obvious descriptions of the sublime and argue that the "sublime settings in the text [...] provide a space where the marginalized can be heard" (Fredericks 1996). Fredericks goes on by saying that the sublime thereby "opens the way for the excluded to challenge the dominant discourse." (ibid.) The concept of beauty, on the other hand, according to her, hands an explanation for Victor's abandonment of the monster, as well as for the monsters role as an outcast and in consequence its violence and longing for revenge. (cf. ibid.)

Fredericks, as mentioned, argues that "the sublime appears as a type of place, represented by the Alps, the Arctic, and the stormy and rugged shores of Scotland. The sublime represents the frontier of human society. The sublime setting is the home of the monster." (ibid.) When looking at scenes 3. to 5. of the appendix, it can be argued that this assumption upholds. Scene 4. shows the first encounter of Frankenstein and the monster. It basically shows Frankenstein's sleeping in his bedroom after creating the monster. The monster tries to

8

reach out to his creator, but Frankenstein turns away as he is clearly appalled by the monsters horrible appearance. The callow monster then must have taken off while Frankenstein escapes and wanders off. (cf. Shelley 1994: 56) The scene is not only essential for the plot development as it starts of the line of events but also bears sublime elements as described by Burke. (cf. Fredericks 1996) It also supports the argument that from his creation on, the monster appears in the majority of cases in sublime settings, for example, as scene 1. from the appendix shows he is "hanging among the rocks of the nearby perpendicular" (Shelley 1994: 73). (cf. Fredericks 1996) Or, even more distinct, the monster even lives among the sublime. The monster set up a camp on the mountain where he brings Frankenstein to discuss his demands. (cf. appendix scene "3. Face-to-face encounter with the monster on the glacier") As Giacomoni puts it, "the creature appears to be perfectly at ease among the crevasses, living among the caverns and the icebergs." (Giacomoni : 120)

The monster's role of an outcast, habituating sublime settings, is even further supported by Frankenstein's description of the mountain landscape in text abstract (6). Victor describes the effect the Alps have on him as that they let him think that they are "belonging to another earth" (Shelley 1994: 90) and furthermore are "the habitation of another race of beings." (ibid.) This, as Giacomoni argues, supports the role of the monster – actually living amongst the Alp at this time – as an outcast. (cf. Giacomoni 2008: 120)

Also, the last scene, the monster's farewell (cf. appendix "5. The monster's farewell at the end of the novel"), supports this argumentation. The monster, first, communicates his intention of killing himself in the arctic realm. Afterwards, he vanishes into the realm, leaving the reader questioning whether he actually kills himself or not. But despite the end being left open, it can be stated that he merges into the arctic realm, "he was [...] lost in the darkness and distance" (Shelley 1994: 215). (cf. Fredericks 1996) Fredericks, furthermore states that in the arctic realm Frankenstein and the monster "are on equal ground." (ibid.) She also argues that Victor has a terrible disadvantage not being at home in sublime settings, especially in the arctic realm. As a consequence, he dies. The monster is clearly superior among the sublime settings because, as Giacomoni puts it, "[t]hese places are unsuitable to the presence of man" (Giacomoni 2008: 120). (cf. Fredericks 1996; cf. Giacomoni 2008: 120) Here it is also interesting to mention that Victor and Walton are in some way similar as they both push beyond the limits of nature and try to encounter the sublime settings. (cf. Fredericks 1996)

Fredericks furthermore states that "[a]gainst the backdrop of the Swiss Alps, Shelley orchestrates a dramatic shift in the reader's sympathy when she allows the monster to tell his side of the story, a woeful tale of neglect and abuse" (ibid.). The sublime setting is the ground

9

for Victor and the excluded to "engage in a dialogue" (ibid.). And, for Victor, the setting also is where sees "his own limitations in the face of the 'other'" (ibid.).

Furthermore, as Alison Milbank argues, from this encounter on,

"For Frankenstein the natural sublime of the glacier becomes horrible, as it brings him no imaginative expansion but the icy recognition of the demands of his monster, a horror made literally frozen in the final scenes of their encounter at the North Pole, which is as much a landscape of the horrible as the Alps are of the sublime." (Milbank 1998: 230)

Whereas the monster is superior in the sublime setting, his desire for acceptance and companionship will not be fulfilled. One of the consequences of locating the monster among the sublime is that Burke's concept of beauty must be taken into account as well. In this matter, Fredericks argues that the monster's lack of beauty, as discussed in length, makes it an outcast. (cf. Fredericks 1996) Fredericks goes on and argues that accordingly one source of the monsters rage is being excluded from having a mate. Here, Burke's theory of beauty plays an important role. Nearly all women in *Frankenstein* are described as beautiful to at least some degree. Victor's Elizabeth even is described as having not much else to her than being beautiful. (cf. ibid.)

In conclusion, it can be stated that the Alpine setting conveys a large portion of the sublime. It is portrait as a sublime setting, as are the arctic real and glacier. Furthermore, the exclusion from beauty is also part of the rage and anger. This exclusion marginalizes the monster and ultimately forces it into the sublime settings. (cf. ibid.)

4. CONCLUSION

The term paper presented here set out to examine how Burke's theory of the sublime is reflected in Mary Shelley's *Frankenstein*. In general, it can be stated that the sublime as an important feature of Gothic fiction, based on a mixed emotion, called 'delight'. (cf. Weber 1983: 26) Furthermore it builds the base for the evoking powerful feelings in the reader. (cf. Sage 1998: 82) Mary Shelley by writing *Frankenstein* actually set out to provoke this effect in the reader as she states in her Introduction to the novel from 1831. (cf. Shelley 1994: 7 – 8) When looking at the sublime in comparison to the beautiful, one can state that the sublime in general is located in humans need for self-preservation, whereas the beautiful is "a social passion" (Sambrook 1986: 121). The beautiful furthermore is an essential quality needed in every society. (cf. Weber 1983: 28)

The novel *Frankenstein* obviously conveys the Burkean sense of the sublime. This is especially true with regard to the description of nature presented in the novel. Here, in particular the Alpine landscape, the glacier and the arctic realm should be mentioned. These settings clearly reflect Burke's theory of the natural sublime. Furthermore, these sublime settings stage as the habitat of Victor Frankenstein's monster. (cf. Fredericks 1996) The concept of beauty, on the other, appears to be giving an explanation for the creature's anger. The exclusion of the monster due to his ugliness ultimately let it merge into the sublime at the very end of the novel. (cf. ibid.) It might even be argued that the creature thereby becomes part of the sublime. For Victor, the sublime is somehow challenging; he sets out to explore the boundaries of nature. But he ultimately fails. He underlies the concept of beauty as all humans do. Victor rejects his creation due to the sheer ugliness. He, furthermore, is not able to live outside society and in the sublime settings and dies in the arctic realm. (cf. ibid.) To answer the initial question: it can be concluded that Shelley's Frankenstein clearly reflects Burke's theory of the sublime.

Although the literature used in this term paper suggest such an argument, it is important not to overlook that the argumentation could also been seen critically. As a result, this term paper suggests a number of further avenues for research; for example, one tentative proposal might be that a study should set out to do a more detailed analysis of the book, taking into account all scenes. Furthermore, the Burkean concept of beauty could be researched in length. Also, with regard to the course, this term paper arose out; one might look at how other features of the Gothic novel are reflected in *Frankenstein*. This could be the supernatural, the uncanny, or horror.

Works Cited

Burke, Edmund. 1757. *A Philosophical Inquiry into the Origins of our Ideas of the Beautiful and the Sublime.* 27.06.2011. <http://www.bartleby.com/24/2/>

Fredricks, Nancy. 1996. On the sublime and beautiful in Shelley's 'Frankenstein. 27.06.2011. <http://www.nsboro.k12.ma.us/algonquin/faculty/englishteachers/coppens/Frankensteincriticalarticle5.html>

Lamb, Jonathan. 1997. "The sublime". In: Nisbet. H.B.; Rawson, Claude, eds. 1997. The Cambridge History of Literary Criticism. Volume 4. The Eighteenth Century.

Giacomoni, Paola. 2008. "Mountain landscape and the aesthetics of the sublime in Romantic narration". In: Gillespie, Gerald et.al., eds. 2008. *Romantic prose fiction. A Comparative History of Literatures in European Languages.* Netherlands/Philadelphia: John Benjamin B.V., pp. 107 – 121.

Martin, Philip W. 1998. "Romanticism". In: Mulvey-Roberts, Marie, eds. 1998. *The Handbook to Gothic Literature.* New York: New York University Press, pp. 195 – 199.

Milbank, Alison. 1998. "The Sublime". In: Mulvey-Roberts, Marie, eds. 1998. *The Handbook to Gothic Literature.* New York: New York University Press, pp. 226 – 232.

Mulvey-Roberts, Marie. 1998. "Shelly, Mary". In: Mulvey-Roberts, Marie, eds. 1998. *The Handbook to Gothic Literature.* New York: New York University Press, pp. 210 – 216.

Sage, Victor. 1998. "Gothic Novel". In: Mulvey-Roberts, Marie, eds. 1998. *The Handbook to Gothic Literature.* New York: New York University Press, pp. 81 – 89.

Sambrook, James. 1986. "Aesthetics". In: Sambrook, James, eds. *The Eighteenth Century. The Intellectual and Cultural Context of English Literature, 1700 – 1789.* New York: Longman, pp. 101 – 133.

Shelly, Mary. 1994. *Frankenstein. Or, The Modern Prometheus.* London: Penguin Books.

Weber, Ingeborg. 1983. "Edmund Burkes Ästhetik des Erhabenen als Gattungspoetik des englischen Schauerromans". In: Weber, Ingeborg, eds. 1983. *Der Englische Schauerroman.* München: Artemis, pp. 20 – 32.

1. QUOTATIONS FROM MARY SHELLEY'S FRANKENSTEIN

The text abstracts are sorted chronologically by use in this term paper, not by appearance in the book. Also, the quotations are all indented for reasons of uniformity, even though some are not longer than three lines.

1. ENCOUNTER OF VICTOR AND THE MONSTER ON HIS RETURN TO GENEVA AFTER HIS BROTHER WILLIAM WAS FOUND MURDERED

(1) **"My country, my beloved country**! Who but a native can **tell the delight I took in again beholding thy streams, thy mountains, and more than all, thy lovely lake**.
Yet as I drew nearer home, grief and fear overcame me. Night also closed around, and when I could hardly see the **dark mountains, I felt still more gloomily**. The picture appeared a vast and dim scene of evil [.]" (Shelley 1994: 72; emphasis mine, A.K.)

(3) "As I could not pass through the town, I was obliged to cross the lake in a boat to arrive at Plainpalais. During this short voyage I saw the **lightnings playing on the summit of Mont Blanc** in the **most beautiful figures**." (Shelley 1994: 72; emphasis mine, A.K.)

(4) "While I watched the tempest, **so beautiful, yet terrific** [...]" (Shelley 1994: 73; emphasis mine, A.K.)

(5) "I perceived in the gloom a figure which stole from behind a clump of trees near me; I stood fixed, gazing intently: I could not be mistaken. **A flash of lightning illuminated the object**, and discovered its shape plainly to me; its **gigantic stature, and the deformity of its aspect, more hideous than belongs to humanity**, instantly informed me that it was the **wretch**, the **filthy daemon**, to whom I had given life. What did he there? Could he be (I shuddered at the conception) the murderer of my brother? No sooner did that idea cross my imagination, than I became convinced of its truth; my teeth chattered, and I was forced to lean against a tree for support. The figure passed me quickly, and I lost it in the gloom. Nothing in human shape could have destroyed that fair child. He was the murderer! I could not doubt it. The mere presence of the idea was an irresistible proof of the fact. I thought of pursuing the **devil**, but it would have been in vain, for **another flash discovered him to me hanging among the rocks of the nearly perpendicular ascent of Mont Saleve, a hill that bounds Plainpalais on the south. He soon reached the summit and disappeared.**" (Shelley 1994: 73; emphasis mine, A.K.)

2. TRAVEL TO THE GLACIER

(6) "The **immense mountains** and precipices that overhung me on every side – the **sound of the river raging among the rocks, and the dashing of the waterfalls around, spoke of a power mighty as Omnipotence – and I ceased to fear**, or to end before any being less **almighty** than that which had **created and ruled the elements**, here displayed in her most terrific guise. Still, as I ascended higher, the valley assumed a more **magnificent** and **astonishing character**. **Ruined castles hanging on the precipices of piny mountains**, the **impetuous Arve**, and cottages every here and there peeping forth from among the trees, formed a scene of singular beauty. But **it was augmented and rendered sublime by the mighty Alps**, whose **white and shining pyramids and domes** towered above all, as belonging to another earth, the habitations of another race of beings." (Shelley 1994: 90; emphasis mine, A.K.)

(7) "I passed the bridge of Pélissier, where the ravine, which the river forms, opened before me, and I began to ascend the mountain that overhangs it. Soon after I entered the valley of Chamounix. **This valley is more wonderful and sublime, but not so beautiful and picturesque, as that of Servox**, through which I had just passed. **The high and snowy mountains** were its immediate boundaries; but I saw no more ruined castles and fertile fields. **Immense glaciers approached the road**; I heard the **rumbling thunder of the falling avalanche**, and marked the smoke of its passage. Mont Blanc, the **supreme and magnificent Mont Blanc**, raised itself from the surrounding *aiguilles*, and its **tremendous dome** overlooked the valley." (Shelley 1994: 90 – 91; emphasis mine, A.K.)

3. FACE-TO-FACE ENCOUNTER WITH THE MONSTER ON THE TOP OF THE GLACIER

(8) "**These sublime and magnificence scenes afforded me the greatest consolation that I was capable of receiving. They elevated me from all littleness of feeling**, and although they did not remove my grief, they subdued and tranquillized it. In some degree, also, **they diverted my mind from the thoughts** over which it had brooded for the last month. (Shelley 1994: 92; emphasis mine, A.K.)

(9) "It was nearly noon when I arrived at the top of the ascent. For some time I sat upon the rock that overlooks the sea of ice. A mist covered both that and the surrounding mountains. Presently a breeze dissipated the cloud, and I descended upon the glacier. **The surface is very uneven, rising like the waves of a troubled sea, descending low, and interspersed by rifts that sink deep**. The field of ice is almost a league in width, but I spent nearly two hours in crossing it. The opposite mountain is a bare perpendicular rock. From the side where I now stood Montanvert was exactly opposite, at the distance of a league, and **above it rose Mont Blanc, in awful majesty**. I remained in a recess of the rock, gazing on this **wonderful and stupendous scene**. The sea, or rather the **vast river of ice, wound among its dependent mountains**, whose aerial summits hung over its

15

recesses. Their **icy and glittering peaks shone in the sunlight** over the clouds. My heart, which was before sorrowful, now swelled with something like joy; I exclaimed – 'Wandering spirits, if indeed ye wander, and do not rest in your narrow beds, allow me this faint happiness, or take me, as your companion, away from the joys of life.'

As I said this, **I suddenly beheld the figure of a man, at some distance, advancing towards me with superhuman speed.** He bounded over the crevices in the ice, among which I had walked with caution; his stature, also, as he approached, seemed to exceed that of man. I was troubled: a mist came over my eyes, and **I felt a faintness seize me; but I was quickly restored by the cold gale of the mountains.** I perceived, as the shape came nearer (**sight tremendous and abhorred!**) that it was the wretch whom I had created. **I trembled with rage and horror**, resolving to wait his approach, and then close with him in mortal combat. He approached; his countenance bespoke bitter, anguish, combined with disdain and malignity, while **its unearthly ugliness** rendered it **almost too horrible for human eyes.** But I scarcely observed this; rage and hatred had at first deprived me of utterance, and I recovered only to overwhelm him with words expressive of furious detestation and contempt." (Shelley 1994: 94 – 95; emphasis mine, A.K.)

(10) "[']Hear my tale; it is long and strange, and the temperature of this place is not fitting to your fine sensations; come to **the hut upon the mountain.**[']" (Shelley 1994: 97; emphasis mine, A.K.)

4. FIRST ENCOUTER OF MONSTER AND CREATOR

(11) "I thought I saw Elizabeth, in the bloom of health, walking in the streets of Ingolstadt. Delighted and surprised, I embraced her; but as I imprinted the first kiss on her lips, they became livid with the hue of death; her features appeared to change, and I thought that I held the **corpse of my dead mother in my arms**; a shroud enveloped her form, and I saw the **grave-worms crawling in the folds of the flannel.** I started from my sleep with horror; a cold dew covered my forehead, my teeth chattered, and every limb became convulsed: when, by the **dim and yellow light of the moon**, as it forced its way through the window shutters, I beheld **the wretch – the miserable monster** whom I had created. He held up the curtain of the bed; and his eyes, if eyes they may be called, were fixed on me. His jaws opened, and he muttered some inarticulate sounds, while a grin wrinkled his cheeks. He might have spoken, but I did not hear; one hand was stretched out, seemingly to detain me, but I escaped, and rushed down stairs. I took refuge in the courtyard belonging to the house which I inhabited; where I remained during the rest of the night, walking up and down in the greatest agitation, listening attentively, catching and fearing each sound as if it were to announce the approach of the **demoniacal corpse** to which I had so miserably given life." (Shelley 1994: 56; emphasis mine, A.K.)

5. THE MONSTER'S FAREWELL AT THE END OF THE NOVEL

(12) "'But soon,' he cried with sad and solemn enthusiasm, 'I shall die, and what I now feel be no longer felt. Soon these burning miseries will be extinct. I shall ascend my funeral pile triumphantly, and exult in the agony of the torturing flames. The light of that conflagration will fade away; my ashes will be swept into the sea by the winds. My spirit will sleep in peace, or if it thinks, it will not surely think thus. Farewell.'

He sprung from the cabin-window, as he said this, upon the ice raft <sic> which lay close to the vessel. He was soon borne away by the waves, and lost in darkness and distance." (Shelley 1994: 215; emphasis mine, A.K.)